PITCH PERFECT: THE ULTIMATE GUIDE TO MARKETING YOUR CAMPGROUND

Brian Searl

Insider Perks, Inc.
2515 Jay Avenue #102
Cleveland, OH 44113

CONTENTS

Introduction

Camping under the stars. S'mores by the campfire. Kayaking across a tranquil lake. For many, these idyllic scenes represent the perfect summer getaway. As more people look to escape crowded cities and connect with nature, campgrounds have become a popular vacation choice. In 2021 alone, campground occupancy rates reached all-time highs.

With rising demand comes increased competition. Stand out in a crowded market by implementing proven marketing strategies designed specifically for campgrounds. This book will guide you through research-backed methods to attract your ideal customers.

We'll start by identifying who your best customers are and what motivates them, through developing customer personas and surveying campers. With insight into your audience, you can craft targeted messaging across the right marketing channels. Ongoing analysis will help you continuously adapt to ever-changing trends in the camping market.

Follow this playbook to fill those campsites and upgrade amenities. Hosting happy campers is rewarding in its own right, but smart marketing will also lead to a thriving business. The journey begins with understanding your customers. Let's get started!

Chapter 1 will provide concrete steps to get inside the minds of different camper segments through customer persona development and market research. With this foundation of knowledge, you'll be equipped to create marketing strategies with true resonance.

CHAPTER 1: KNOW YOUR AUDIENCE

Introduction

They say the customer is always right. But how can you make your customers happy if you don't know who they are? Successfully marketing your campground starts with identifying your target audience.

Developing fictional customer personas will help you represent your ideal customers and understand what motivates them. Back up assumptions about your audience with concrete market research. Surveys, interviews, and reviews can provide valuable insights to guide your marketing strategy.

This chapter will cover:

Creating detailed customer personas based on demographics and psychographics
Conducting primary market research through surveys
Analyzing research data to identify promising customer segments
Using personas and research to inform marketing decisions
Follow these steps to get a clear picture of your customers. You'll be ready to reach them with resonating messages tailored to their wants and needs.

Section 1: Identifying Customer Personas

Subsection 1.1: What is a Customer Persona?

A customer persona is a fictional representation of your ideal target audience. Personas go beyond basic demographics to paint a holistic picture of customer beliefs, motivations, and behaviors. They help humanize market segments for easier marketing.

Personas should be based on real data about existing and potential customers. However, they are idealized profiles, not exact customer duplicates. The goal is to capture major wants, needs, and characteristics you can target.

Well-developed personas provide numerous benefits:

Guide marketing content and messaging
Focus product development on customer needs
Support customer-centric business decisions
Represent target segments in internal discussions
With personas in mind, you can craft marketing resonating with precisely who you aim to serve.

Subsection 1.2: Core Demographics

Demographic details like age, gender, income, and location form the foundation of accurate personas. Consider collecting:

Age ranges
Percentage of couples vs. families vs. singles
Average household income
Home geographic region
For instance, a campground may see demand from higher-income families and retired couples. Both are promising targets.

Subsection 1.3: Psychographics

Layer in psychographic details to give personas real depth:

Lifestyle - Active? Outdoor enthusiasts? Luxury travelers?
Interests - Fishing? Hiking? Birdwatching?
Values - Family-oriented? Eco-conscious? Budget-focused?
Psychographics reveal shared mindsets and behaviors tied to demographic groups. For example, older travelers may share a slower paced, comfort-focused trip style.

Subsection 1.4: Types of Campers

Categorizing customers by camper type can inform persona frameworks:

Family campers - Often middle-income parents with younger kids looking for fun, family bonding.

Adventure seekers - Crossover interests from hiking to kayaking. Willing to rough it to challenge themselves.

Festival goers - Camping serves as inexpensive lodging for multi-day music/arts festivals.

Seasonal snowbirds - Retirees who travel south annually and stay awhile. Seek community.

Consider the characteristics and trip motivations typical of each group. What types frequent your campground?

Subsection 1.5: Persona Creation Case Study

Let's walk through an example persona for a fictional campground attracting families and outdoor enthusiasts.

First, core demographics:

Ages 30-45
Mix of married couples and families
Upper-middle income
Located within 1-2 hours drive
Now, psychographics:

Active lifestyle
Appreciation of nature
Interest in outdoor activities like kayaking, hiking, biking
Seek quality family time
With this foundation, we can build a persona narrative:

Meet John and Jane Smith, both 35 years old with a son, age 8, and daughter, age 5. As an upper-middle class family living in the suburbs, they look for ways to escape the city and bond outdoors. They enjoy activities like kayaking, swimming, and hiking. As concerned parents, they seek a family-friendly campground providing a safe, comfortable trip experience with amenities like clean bathrooms, recreation areas for kids, and scenic natural beauty.

Section 2: Market Research and Surveys

Subsection 2.1: Importance of Market Research

Assumptions can be dangerous - the persona creation process should be backed by market research. Collecting primary data directly from your target market is invaluable for confirming you have the right customer segments in focus.

Key benefits of conducting primary market research include:

Validating assumed target audiences and personas
Identifying gaps between your perceptions and reality
Gathering customer feedback to strengthen marketing
Monitoring changes in audience interests and behaviors over time
Make research an ongoing effort. Continuously collecting first-hand data ensures your strategies evolve along with your customers.

Subsection 2.2: Conducting Surveys

Well-designed surveys provide a wealth of market insights from current and potential customers. Consider distributing surveys via:

Your website
Email newsletter signups
Social media
Printed handouts for campers on-site
Keep surveys concise at 5-10 questions. Start with basic demographic inquiries before moving into psychographic interests, values, and motivations. Pay attention to question order

and flow. Close with an open-ended prompt inviting additional feedback.

Subsection 2.3: Data Analysis

Once collected, survey data should be analyzed to reveal:

Primary customer demographics
Psychographic patterns and shared attitudes
Reasons for choosing your campground
Desired amenities and areas for improvement
Organize results in user-friendly dashboards. Quantify data like age brackets and geographic regions. Also identify key themes from open-ended questions. Are families interested in more children's activities? This analysis informs marketing priorities.

Subsection 2.4: Feedback Mechanisms

Supplement periodic surveys with always-on feedback channels:

Monitoring reviews on platforms like Google, Yelp, and Facebook
Sending post-stay feedback emails with quick rating scales
Empowering staff to gather on-site customer feedback
Proactively collecting reviews and critiques provides regular qualitative data from real customers in their own words. Mine this feedback for marketing insights.

Section 3: Putting It All Together

Subsection 3.1: Segmentation and Targeting

With personas validated through market research, you can identify your most viable audience segments. Assess potential targets based on:

Accessibility - Can you reach this group? Do they visit your geographic area?

Profitability - Will targeting this segment deliver revenue that exceeds additional marketing costs?

Then tailor messaging and offers to resonate. For family campers, emphasize kid-friendly activities. For retirees, focus on relaxation and community. Aligning marketing to persona interests boosts conversions.

Subsection 3.2: Communication Channels

Research channels where your target personas spend time, both online and offline. Families may be most active on Facebook, while retirees still read printed newspapers and brochures.

Promote across the right mix of channels to intercept your audience. Adjust over time as their habits and technological proficiency changes.

Subsection 3.3: Continuous Learning

The camping market evolves constantly. Refresh personas annually with new survey data. Watch for demographic and psychographic shifts.

For example, younger adventure travelers may replace some retirees over time. This impacts marketing - these groups consume different media and respond to different messaging.

Regular market check-ins ensure you keep attracting the most relevant customer segments as the market transforms.

Summary

Knowing your target audience is the foundation of campground marketing success. This chapter provided strategies to:

Develop fictional but data-driven customer personas with demographic and psychographic details

Conduct primary market research through surveys to validate assumptions

Analyze results to identify the most viable audience segments to target

Use personas and research learnings to craft targeted, relevant marketing

With these steps, you're ready to promote your campground in a way that deeply resonates with your guests. Get ready for happy campers and a memorable trip experience for all.

CHAPTER 2:
BRANDING YOUR
CAMPGROUND

Introduction

A strong brand is invaluable for campground marketing success. Your brand encompasses your name, logo, messaging, customer service, and the overall image projected to customers. It's the sum total of their perceptions.

Crafting a consistent, recognizable brand allows prospective guests to know what to expect from their stay. It builds trust and memorability. This chapter will explore key steps to develop and maintain a compelling campground brand over time.

We'll cover:

Selecting your campground's name, slogan, and logo to reflect your unique identity.

Building brand recognition through visual identity, online presence, and messaging.

Ensuring brand consistency through customer service and reviews monitoring.

Adapting your brand through periodic audits and refresh based on market research.

Follow this in-depth playbook to craft a brand that attracts your ideal campers and delivers on what you promise.

Section 1: Developing Your Campground Brand DNA

Your campground's name, slogan, logo, and mission statement form the core of your brand identity. These elements should clearly convey who you are and what you offer.

Subsection 1.1: Selecting Your Name and Slogan

Your campground name is your first touchpoint with potential customers. A memorable, evocative name has power. Considerations for your name include:

Descriptiveness - Does it communicate your key features or values? Names like Lakeside Campground or Mountain Ridge RV Park identify location and amenities.

Distinction - Steer clear of overused names by brainstorming creative options or phrases.

Length - Shorter names are best for ease of memory and signage.

Availability - Search online and conduct trademark research to ensure your name doesn't already exist.

Pair your name with a catchy slogan or tagline. For example, "Lakeside Campground: Where Family Memories Are Made." Reinforce your unique positioning.

Subsection 1.2: Crafting Your Mission Statement

Your mission statement summarizes your campground's reason for being. It captures your core goals and principles. An effective mission statement is:

Concise - Generally 3-4 sentences or less.

Memorable - Uses vivid language.

Inspiring - Conveys passion and purpose.

Distinctive - Communicates your competitive advantage.

Example mission statement:

Sunny Days Campground provides a magical outdoor escape for families and adventurers. With picturesque natural scenery and amenities for all ages, we create lasting memories to treasure for a lifetime. Experience the magic of the outdoors with us!

Subsection 1.3: Designing Your Logo

A versatile logo is the cornerstone of your visual brand identity. Consider key logo design principles:

Simplicity - Clean, straightforward graphics stand out. Avoid clutter.

Symbolism - Incorporate visual motifs that represent your campground, like trees, mountains, etc.

Memorability - Use one or two distinctive colors. Lean on familiar shapes.

Adaptability - The logo should translate well large or small, print or digital.

Consistency - Resist redesigning frequently. Build equity over time.

Draft multiple logo concepts. Socialize internally and with customers to select the best option.

Section 2: Building Brand Recognition

Consistency strengthens branding across touchpoints. Maintain alignment with your visual identity, online platforms, and messaging.

Subsection 2.1: Maintaining Visual Identity

Create graphic standards for using logo variations, fonts, colors, and imagery. Produce templates for brochures, signage, website, and more. This ensures a cohesive look.

Your style guide should cover areas such as:

Logo usage - minimum size, exclusion zone, color versions

Typography - approved display and body fonts

Color palettes - primary and secondary colors for all applications

Photo selection - style, filters, motifs that represent your brand

Graphic elements - badges, borders, icons to incorporate

Provide resources like style guides, logos, and photography assets to anyone producing campground communications.

Subsection 2.2: Curating Your Online Presence

Your website and listings on booking/review sites shape perceptions. Ensure your online presence aligns with branding.

Consolidate websites to avoid fragmentation. Visitors should not be confused about which site is official.

Design your website to reflect visual identity. Optimize photos and text for SEO.

Select domains that match your name (.com if available) for findability.

Curate and update robust campground listings on TripAdvisor, Google, Facebook, and similar platforms. Monitor reviews.

Subsection 2.3: Promoting Unified Messaging

Identify 3-5 brand pillars - the core principles and attributes to highlight across communications. For example: family-friendly, comfort, activities, natural beauty, relaxation.

Craft marketing messages and content tailored to resonate with each target audience segment's interests. Occasionally weave in your brand slogan.

Subsection 2.4: Ensuring On-Brand Customer Service

Guest interactions can make or break brand perceptions. Hire campground staff aligned with your brand principles. Train them on ideal service standards. Empower them to promptly resolve issues to delight guests.

Monitor guest feedback and reviews. Look for common themes about strengths or problem areas affecting brand reputation. Continuously improve.

Section 3: Evaluating and Evolving Your Brand

Regular tune-ups keep your brand current amidst changing camping trends.

Subsection 3.1: Brand Audits and Refresh

Set a reminder to formally evaluate your brand elements every 2-3 years. Assess:

Name - Does it still resonate? Would a refresh better convey your brand?

Logo - Is it dated? Should it be modernized while retaining equity?

Visual identity - Do website, signage, etc. need updated design?

Messaging - Do your brand pillars still make sense?

Refresh outdated elements while maintaining familiar core equities. Budget annually for brand reinvestment. Small improvements have big impact.

Subsection 3.2: Adapting Your Brand Strategy

Evolve your focus along with changes in the camping market. Monitor shifts in your audience makeup and interests. Identify rising amenities or trip styles.

Pivot your brand identity to remain relevant, while upholding legacy brand elements that built equity over the years. Your adaptations should reflect market trends.

Subsection 3.3: Repositioning Your Brand

In cases of extreme brand deprecation, a complete rebrand may be prudent. Warning signs include:

Your name or concept grew outdated or negative

Competitors out-innovated you

Offerings no longer match audience expectations

Significant loss of market share

Execute a new name, logo, identity and messaging aligned with redefined target segments. Implement across touchpoints to relaunch as a revitalized brand.

Conclusion

A compelling campground brand makes a promise that your actual offerings must fulfill. By developing a consistent identify with periodic refresh, you attract loyal guests who know what to expect. They become de facto brand advocates referring friends and family.

CHAPTER 3: DIGITAL REAL ESTATE

Introduction

Your online presence across websites, search engines, review platforms, and social media forms the digital foundation of your campground marketing. Optimizing your digital real estate establishes visibility and credibility with modern travelers who plan vacations through internet research and reservations.

This chapter will explore key digital channels, providing actionable steps to:

Create an effective campground website optimized for conversions

Improve search engine rankings through on-page and off-page optimization

Manage robust listings on review sites like TripAdvisor and Google

Drive brand awareness on social media platforms ideal for your audience

Develop email marketing strategies to nurture leads

Follow this comprehensive playbook to maximize your campground's digital footprint across critical channels. Your online presence will become an asset driving growth.

Section 1: Your Campground Website

Your website is the hub of your digital marketing ecosystem. An optimized site captures new visitors and persuades them to book.

Subsection 1.1: Selecting a Domain

Your domain name should match your campground name or branding where possible. Strive for:

Short and memorable
Easy to spell and say aloud
Uses common extensions like .com
Buy all variations - .com, .net, .org to prevent duplication. Redirect them to your primary domain.

Subsection 1.2: Working with Web Developers

Partner with web developers to build an effective site aligned with your brand identity and target audience interests. Look for:

Strong portfolio of campground or hospitality sites
Experience with UX design, conversion optimization
Familiarity with booking integrations
SEO best practices expertise
Provide brand assets like logos and outline your goals, target audience, and desired functionality.

Subsection 1.3: Key Pages and Content

Ensure your website covers essential pages and content:

Homepage - Hero visuals, value proposition, calls to action
Accommodations - Photos, descriptions, pricing and availability
Amenities - Details and images of key amenities
Activities - Lists of recreation opportunities onsite and nearby
Contact - Reservations process, phone numbers, email access
About Us - Your campground story and team bios
Blog or News - For fresh content and SEO
All pages should speak to your brand identity and visitor interests.

Subsection 1.4: Optimizing for Conversions

Optimize website copy, layouts, and calls-to-action for conversions:

Include a strong value proposition explaining why visitors should choose your campground.

Make booking and contact options obvious.

Limit competing navigation and distractions to funnel visitors towards conversions.

Display trust symbols like security seals.

Feature guest reviews and social proof.

Subsection 1.5: Integrating Your Booking System

Work with your booking system provider to embed reservation functionality directly within your website for convenient booking. Offer:

Real-time availability with dynamic rates and dates.

An online reservation form or shopping cart experience.

Instant confirmations and guest account creation.

Subsection 1.6: Updating and Maintaining Your Site

Revisit your website periodically to:

Add new photos and content.

Update rates and inventory availability.

Refresh branding or layouts.

Fix broken links, errors, or problems.

Improve speed and conversion rates.

An outdated website frustrates visitors. Budget time for ongoing enhancements.

Section 2: Search Engine Optimization

SEO improves visibility in search engines like Google to drive traffic to your site. Core optimization strategies include:

Subsection 2.1: On-Page Optimization

On-page signals like keywords help search engines understand your content and rankings:

Page titles and headings - Insert relevant keywords.

URL structure - Descriptive URLs with keywords aid indexing.

Image optimization - Descriptive file names and alt text improve image SEO.

Target key phrases - Focus on phrases travelers search when planning camps.

Craft unique meta descriptions to compel clicks.

Subsection 2.2: Off-Page Optimization

Off-page signals come from other sites linking to yours:

Link building - Reach out to partners, directories, and influencers to acquire backlinks.

Social media - Link to your website from all social profiles.

Listings -Claim and optimize campground directory listings which link back to your site.

Monitor search rankings - Track rankings for target phrases over time to gauge improvements.

Section 3: Review Site Listings

Active listings on major review platforms drive valuable organic traffic.

Subsection 3.1: Claiming and Managing Listings

Claim and flesh out your campground profiles on key sites like:

Google My Business
TripAdvisor
Yelp
Facebook
Completing descriptions, adding photos, and responding to reviews signals you actively manage the listing, leading to better placements.

Subsection 3.2: Responding to Reviews

Reply promptly to all reviews, especially negative critiques. Thank guests for feedback. Explain how you'll improve shortcomings. Reviews show you care.

Subsection 3.3: Encouraging New Reviews

Prompt happy guests to leave reviews with:

Follow-up emails after their stay
Signage and QR codes on-site
Contests and giveaways for reviewers
The more reviews, the more visible and credible your listings appear.

Section 4: Social Media Marketing

An active social media presence keeps your brand top of mind with current and potential guests.

Subsection 4.1: Selecting Platforms

Base your platform mix on where your audience engages:

Facebook remains ideal for broad consumer demographics.

Instagram and Pinterest suit visually focused camps.

Twitter works for real-time conversation.

Avoid spreading efforts thin. Start with your core channels.

Subsection 4.2: Crafting Engaging Content

Post a steady mix of content like:

Professional photos of your grounds, accommodations, views, amenities and activities

Guest pictures and testimonials

Promotions and special offers

Polls, questions, and contests to generate engagement

Stay on-brand. Use relevant hashtags. Tag partners.

Subsection 4.3: Paid Ads

Consider small paid campaigns to expand reach for promotions. Target by interests and geography. Test conversions across platforms. Add budget slowly.

Subsection 4.4: Contests and Promotions

Contests, giveaways, and hashtags build awareness while collecting emails and UGC. For example:

Share photos of your stay for a chance to win a free night

Use hashtag #YourCampgroundName for a follow

Section 5: Email Marketing

Email nurtures leads and past guests. Send promotions, newsletters, and automated campaigns.

Subsection 5.1: Collecting Emails

Offer incentives for visitors to opt-in to your email list via:

Website pop-ups and signup bars

Social media

Contests

Surveys

Guest receipts

Subsection 5.2: Design and Content

Create emails reflecting brand visual identity. Include:

Promotions, deals, and seasonal offers

Relevant educational content

Campground news and updates

Links to booking

Subsection 5.3: Automated Sequences

Set up automated email workflows like:

Welcome series when subscribers join

Pre-stay confirmations and prep reminders

Post-stay feedback surveys and reviews requests

Win-back promotions for previous guests

Subsection 5.4: Analytics and Optimization

Track email metrics in your CRM like:

Open rates

Clickthrough rates

Conversions

Use insights to refine your strategy and increase performance over time.

Conclusion

Your digital presence hugely impacts campground visibility and success. By optimizing across critical channels presented in this chapter, you attract qualified traffic that converts to reservations.

Key takeaways include:

Developing a high-converting campground website

Improving search rankings through on-page and off-page optimization

Managing robust listings on Google, TripAdvisor, Facebook

Promoting your brand on ideal social media platforms

Building your email list and send targeted campaigns

Committing to long-term digital strategies generates compounding returns over time as your channels grow in authority and reach. Developing a strong digital footprint takes consistent effort, but the ROI is immense.

CHAPTER 4: BUILDING YOUR SOCIAL MEDIA PRESENCE

Introduction

Social media allows campgrounds to directly engage with current and prospective guests. Platforms like Facebook, Instagram, and Twitter provide venues to promote your brand, highlight your property's amenities and activities, and foster a community.

This chapter will provide in-depth guidance on developing an impactful social media presence, including:

Selecting the right platforms and accounts to focus your efforts
Creating engaging social content aligned with brand identity
Utilizing both organic and paid advertising strategies
Leveraging contests, user-generated content, and influencers
Measuring performance through key analytics and insights
Follow this comprehensive playbook to make social media a driver of brand awareness, leads, and bookings for your campground.

Section 1: Choosing Your Social Media Platforms

With so many options, committing to just a few key platforms is best to establish your presence.

Subsection 1.1: Identifying Your Target Audience's Platforms

Research where your ideal campers spend their time online. For most, key platforms include:

Facebook - Broadest demographics with wide adoption makes this a must-have channel.

Instagram - Ideal for visually focused, younger demographics. Drive bookings by showcasing property.

Twitter - Followers look here for real-time updates, news and conversation.

Select platforms already popular with your target audiences to ensure relevancy. You can expand to additional channels once your core platforms thrive.

Subsection 1.2: Your Primary Account

Choose one platform as your primary hub with the most resources allocated to content and community management. This often will be Facebook, but consider your audience insights.

Use your primary account as the anchor for your other social channels. Cross-promote content across platforms to stretch reach.

Subsection 1.3: Consistent Branding

Keep branding consistent across your social accounts:

Identified by campground name
Use matching profile and cover photos
Link to website in bios
Cross-tag accounts in posts
Maintaining the same look and voice builds recognition.

Section 2: Creating Compelling Social Content

Content should educate and entertain followers while conveying your brand identity.

Subsection 2.1: Content Pillars

Identify 4-5 regular content pillars aligned with your brand positioning, such as:

Showcasing grounds, amenities and accommodation photos
Highlighting activities, recreation and area attractions
Featuring special events, holidays and seasonal happenings
Promoting deals, packages and booking incentives
Sharing guest testimonials and user-generated content
Subsection 2.2: Balancing Content Types

Vary content formats to maintain interest:

Vibrant, high-quality photos and videos
Infographics with statistics, tips, or area information
Polls and questions to spark engagement
Written posts showcasing activities, history, or campground news
Live videos giving previews of grounds or behind-the-scenes looks
Subsection 2.3: Engagement Strategies

Employ tactics to increase engagement:

Use relevant hashtags, especially branded tags unique to your campground
Tag partners, attractions, and area organizations
Ask questions and prompt comments
Run weekly contests for shares, likes, or user-generated content
Leverage seasonal hooks and current events
Section 3: Promoting Your Content

Getting content seen by your target audience drives awareness and conversions. Use both organic and paid tactics.

Subsection 3.1: Organic Promotion

Organic promotion leverages channels available at no cost:

Post consistently 1-2 times daily on primary platform
Engage followers by liking, commenting on their posts
Cross-promote across your social platforms
Encourage shares, tags, and mentions by followers
Utilize relevant hashtags, especially branded one for your

campground

Subsection 3.2: Social Media Ads

Paid ads supplement organic reach to get content in front of targeted demographics:

Promote visual assets like campground photos and videos
Boost new offers, discounts, and booking promotions
Retarget past visitors
Set geographic radius within your driveable region
Start with low daily budget; scale up as you measure conversion performance

Subsection 3.3: Influencers and Takeovers

Work with social influencers in your area to create content highlighting camp activities. Also consider hosting an Instagram takeover featuring their account for a day.

Section 4: Contests, UGC, and Reviews

Special initiatives like contests and user-generated content foster higher engagement.

Subsection 4.1: Contests and Giveaways

Contests incentivize followers to engage for a chance to win prizes like:

Free nights or activities
Camp swag like t-shirts, water bottles, etc.
Area attraction tickets
Future discounts
Boost contest posts to drive entries. Capture emails for your database.

Subsection 4.2: User-Generated Content

Encourage followers to tag you in their photos from your campground. Repost the best shots while tagging and crediting the photographer. This shows you listening to your guests. Offer incentives like free merchandise for top contributors.

Subsection 4.3: Reviews

Prompt positive reviews on your profiles. Respond publicly thanking the user. This social proof helps convince potential guests.

Section 5: Analytics and Insights

Robust analytics show what content resonates so you can refine your strategy.

Subsection 5.1: Audience Insights

Review audience demographic data:

Follower count and follower growth rates
Age, gender, location breakdowns
Peak engagement times and days
Subsection 5.2: Performance Reporting

Measure content performance with metrics like:

Reach and impressions
Engagement rate
Clicks, comments, shares, saves
Website referral traffic
Lead conversions
Subsection 5.3: Optimization

Use learnings to guide future content planning:

Identify best-performing content types, topics, and formats to expand
Stop non-performing content that doesn't engage followers
Adjust posting cadence based on peak interaction times
Refine ad targeting and boost top-converting posts
Continuous optimization over time improves results.

Conclusion

A strategic social media presence keeps your campground top of mind while actively converting new leads. Dedicate resources to create compelling content, engage followers, promote actively, and analyze performance.

CHAPTER 5: LOCAL PARTNERSHIPS AND SPONSORSHIPS

Introduction

Forming partnerships with local businesses and organizations benefits campgrounds in multiple ways. Strategic collaborations increase visibility, drive referrals, provide added value to guests, and show your support for the community.

This chapter will explore various types of partnerships, and provide actionable strategies to:

Identify relevant potential partners fitting your brand and offerings
Structure mutually beneficial partnerships emphasizing value exchanges
Activate partnerships through co-marketing campaigns and cross-promotion
Manage ongoing relationships and maximize partnership value
Evaluate and select impactful event or cause sponsorships
Follow this in-depth guide to make partnerships an integral component of your multifaceted campground marketing program.

Section 1: Partnership Opportunities

Many types of local establishments make strong partners. Consider:

Subsection 1.1: Activity Providers

Partner with businesses offering activities complementary to camping like:

Outfitters for fishing, hunting, kayaking, canoeing
Guides for hiking, adventure tours, horseback riding
Marinas and boat rentals
Bike shops for sales, rentals, repairs
Golf courses and country clubs
Subsection 1.2: Food & Beverage

Hospitality businesses include:

Restaurants for casual or fine dining
Breweries, wineries, distilleries
Farms offering fresh produce or U-pick
Orchards and fruit stands
Specialty food shops with local goods
Subsection 1.3: Retailers

Retail partners provide guest essentials:

Grocery stores, markets, convenience stores
Gas stations
Camping and outdoor gear shops
Drug stores and pharmacies
General merchandisers
Subsection 1.4: Events & Attractions

Connect with local sights and happenings:

Amusement parks, zoos, museums, aquariums
State and national parks
Music venues and concert series
Annual fairs, festivals, and events
Farmers markets and craft fairs
Historical sites and landmarks
Subsection 1.5: Tourism Boards

Coordinate with organizations promoting your area:

Convention and visitors bureaus (CVBs)
Local and regional tourism commissions
State tourism office
Chamber of commerce
Section 2: Crafting Mutually Beneficial Partnerships

For long-term success, partnerships must add value for both brands.

Subsection 2.1: Researching Partners

Vet potential partners to confirm they align with your brand and deliver on promises:

Visit business to assess quality, service
Review online reputation and guest sentiment
Ensure they fulfill a guest need not currently addressed
Subsection 2.2: Defining Value Exchanges

Outline specific value each partner brings to the table. Campgrounds can offer:

Exposure to your guests through promotions, referrals, on-site presence
Local market expertise and networking
Event, product, or service packages
Partners can provide:

Discounts and special offers for your guests
Co-marketing through their own channels
Increased reservations and commissions on booked referrals
Presence at your campground for activations
Subsection 2.3: Formalizing Agreements

Outline partnership terms and conditions in writing:

Objectives and value exchange
Activation period and guidelines

Metrics for tracking
Approval processes
Usage rights for logos and trademarks
Contingency plans
This sets clear expectations.

Section 3: Activating and Maintaining Partnerships

Bring partnerships to life through cross-promotion. Steward relationships long-term.

Subsection 3.1: Promoting Partners

Feature partners prominently:

Showcase promotions, specials, and packages on your website and social media
Distribute partner coupons and flyers on-site and via guest communications
Give partners exposure at on-site events or activities
Subsection 3.2: Driving Referrals

Incentivize guests to visit partners with perks like:

Discounts for presenting your campground key tag or receipt
Free extras like dessert, t-shirt, tasting, or add-ons
Points or punch-card for redemptions after visiting multiple partners
Subsection 3.3: Co-Marketing Campaigns

Coordinate campaigns promoting both brands:

Sweepstakes for prizes from both businesses
Hashtag campaigns on social media
Co-branded giveaways and contests
Packages bundling stays with partner offers
Subsection 3.4: Managing Relationships

Steward partnerships proactively:

Check in regularly to address questions

Collect feedback on partnership performance
Troubleshoot any guest or execution issues
Socialize new offerings or changes on both sides
Annually review terms for modifications or renewal
Section 4: Sponsorship Opportunities

Local sponsorships raise awareness while giving back.

Subsection 4.1: Identifying Events

Seek out events aligning with your brand and audience:

Community fundraisers
Campground industry events
Races, concerts, festivals
Environmental causes
Subsection 4.2: Sponsorship Levels

Secure a sponsorship level that maximizes your benefits:

Title sponsor - Highest level, ubiquitous brand visibility
Presenting sponsor - High visibility, sponsor name in event title
Supporting sponsor - Moderate visibility, may sponsor specific portion
Subsection 4.3: Evaluating Events

Vet events on criteria like:

Attendee demographics and projected numbers
Media coverage and promotional plans
Brand alignment - does it fit your positioning?
Past success and professionalism
Sponsor packages and benefits offered
Event location and timing fit
Subsection 4.4: Onsite Activations

Look for opportunities for onsite presence when possible:

Booth for giveaways, lead generation
Product displays or demos

Speaking opportunities
Campground vehicle presence
This raises your profile at the event.

Conclusion

Partnerships with local businesses, events, and organizations provide campgrounds with new marketing channels, value-added offers for guests, brand visibility, and community goodwill.

CHAPTER 6: EMAIL MARKETING

Introduction

Email marketing enables campground owners to directly reach guests and prospects with promotions, updates, surveys, and more. This invaluable digital channel fosters ongoing relationships and conversions when nurtured effectively.

This chapter will explore proven email marketing strategies for campgrounds, with actionable guidance on:

Collecting email addresses through various methods
Designing on-brand, mobile-friendly emails
Developing value-driven educational and promotional email content
Executing targeted campaigns like newsletters, post-stay surveys, and holiday promotions
Automating segmented workflows such as welcome series, abandoned booking nudges, and win-back campaigns
Monitoring key email metrics to optimize deliverability, open rates, and engagement over time
Follow this comprehensive playbook to make email marketing a pillar driving bookings, reviews, referrals and revenue growth for your campground year-round.

Section 1: Building Your Email List

Growing your email subscriber list lays the foundation for email success. Capture emails through:

Subsection 1.1: Website Integration

Add email signup forms or popups across your website:

Homepage
Contact and FAQ pages
Resource library gated access
Booking confirmation pages
Contest landing pages
Offer a lead magnet like a guide, checklist, or savings coupon to incentivize signups.

Subsection 1.2: Social Media

Promote email signup giveaways and contests on social channels. Share signup links in your social media bios.

Subsection 1.3: Surveys

Close each survey with an option to subscribe for news and promotions.

Subsection 1.4: Contests

Run contests where entrants provide their email address to enter giveaways.

Subsection 1.5: Guest Receipts

Print your mailing list signup link on guest receipts. Offer a discount on their next booking for signing up.

Subsection 1.6: Legal Requirements

Always include an unsubscribe link, postal address, and opt-in confirmation to align with anti-spam laws like CAN-SPAM and GDPR when collecting emails.

Subsection 1.7: CRM Database

Organize all subscriber data in one central CRM or contacts database, segmented by tags like:

Current customers
Past customers
Prospects
Inactive contacts
Proper data hygiene fuels effective ongoing engagement.

Section 2: Designing Effective Emails

Optimize email design, content format, and value delivery for subscribers.

Subsection 2.1: Design Best Practices

Every email should:

Use consistent brand colors, fonts, and logo
Have clear organization and easy-to-scan layouts
Display properly on all devices, especially mobile
Avoid large file sizes that impede load times
Subsection 2.2: Email Content Essentials

Include engaging copy, offers, and relevant visual assets:

Educate subscribers with campground tips, area spotlights, and seasonal content

Promote special offers like discounts, package deals, contests or giveaways

Share updates and news about renovations, new amenities, special events, etc.

Add photos, videos, GIFs to illustrate offers and campground highlights

Insert clear calls-to-action like booking now, claiming an offer, or visiting a page

Subsection 2.3: Professional Email Platforms

Use email service providers like Mailchimp, Constant Contact, or

ConvertKit for professional templates, automation, analytics, and deliverability.

Most integrate with CRMs to sync subscriber data.

Section 3: Targeted Email Campaigns

Send campaigns aligned to subscriber needs at strategic points.

Subsection 3.1: Welcome Emails

Kick off relationship with a welcome series covering:

Appreciation for subscribing

Quick links to explore your site and social media pages

Overview of upcoming news and offers they can expect

Subsection 3.2: Guest Satisfaction Surveys

Request feedback post-stay via email surveys while the trip is still fresh, including:

Overall satisfaction rating

What they enjoyed most

Areas for improvement

Likelihood to return or recommend

Subsection 3.3: Promotions and Deals

Send promotional emails highlighting:

Seasonal packages and events

Holiday weekends or dates with availability

Last-minute deals

Coupon codes and rate discounts

Room upgrade offers

Subsection 3.4: Newsletters

Send monthly newsletters with sections like:

Latest happenings and news

Coming events

Featured guest recipe or experience

Promotional offer

New amenities or planned improvements

Subsection 3.5: Holiday and Seasonal

Add festive flair to promotional emails surrounding:

Holiday weekends
Season openings like spring, summer, or ski season
School holidays when family travel spikes
Oktoberfest, Memorial Day, July 4th, etc.
Subsection 3.6: Retargeting Inactive Contacts

Win back guests who haven't opened in 6+ months with:

"We miss you" subject lines
Surveys asking why they haven't booked
Discounts for reactivation
Section 4: Email Automation

Automate drip campaigns that convert at scale.

Subsection 4.1: Welcome Sequences

Automate a series over 2-3 weeks after signup:

Part 1: Thanks for subscribing
Part 2: Overview of amenities
Part 3: Special offer incentive to book
Subsection 4.2: Post-Stay Surveys

Trigger a feedback survey 3-5 days after every stay.

Subsection 4.3: Abandoned Booking Nudges

Remind those who started but didn't complete an online booking to finish reserving.

Subsection 4.4: Win-Back Campaigns

Re-engage inactive subscribers who haven't opened in 6+ months.

Subsection 4.5: Birthday and Anniversary Messages

Delight guests by recognizing special occasions.

Subsection 4.6: Transactional Emails

Systematically send booking confirmations, pre-arrival tips, invoices, and other transactional messages.

Section 5: Measurement and Optimization

Key metrics reveal what works to refine your approach.

Subsection 5.1: Open and Clickthrough Rates

Gauge engagement levels by list segment - aim for:

Above 20% open rate
2-5% clickthrough rate
Subsection 5.2 Conversion Tracking

Understand conversions driven by:

Traffic to your website
Bookings
Offer claims
Survey submission
Subsection 5.3: List Growth

Monitor your list size and growth over time. Set lead gen goals.

Subsection 5.4: Unsubscribe Rate

Keep an eye on opt-outs. Excessive unsubscribes may signal deliverability issues or irrelevant content.

Subsection 5.5: Insights and Optimization

Dig into email and integration platform analytics to identify opportunities - what content works? What could be improved? Refine your approach to boost engagement.

Conclusion

Email marketing remains an invaluable channel for cost-efficiently driving conversions and direct relationships with campground guests. This chapter provided data-backed best practices for:

Capturing email addresses through multiple methods

Crafting well-designed, valuable email content

Executing campaigns aligned to guest needs at strategic timing

Automating tailored email sequences and workflows

Monitoring key metrics and optimizing based on insights and performance

By growing your subscriber list and nurturing it with strategic email campaigns over time, you will fill more sites, earn more 5-star reviews, and build lasting guest loyalty.

CHAPTER 7: PAID ADVERTISING

Introduction

While organic marketing through your website, social media, and content is essential for campground visibility, paid advertising accelerates results by putting your brand in front of motivated audiences at scale.

This chapter will explore today's most effective paid channels and tactics to reach your ideal campers, including:

Search engine marketing through Google Ads and Bing Ads
Social media advertising on Facebook, Instagram, and beyond
Display and video advertising across the web
Travel platform ads and listings
Direct mail campaigns
For each channel, we will cover campaign types, targeting capabilities, creative best practices, and performance tracking to maximize your return on ad spend.

Follow this comprehensive playbook to make paid advertising a powerful component of your multimedia campground marketing strategy.

Section 1: Search Engine Marketing

Search ads on Google and Bing put your campground in front of travelers ready to book.

Subsection 1.1: Google Ads

Google Ads offers several ad formats across Google search and Display Network:

Search ads - Text ads next to search results
Display ads - Graphical ads on websites and videos
Video ads - Promoted videos on YouTube and partners
Subsection 1.2: Bing Ads

Bing Ads provides similar options for search ads and native ads across Bing, Yahoo, and partner networks.

Subsection 1.3: Keyword Research

Research and bid on searched phrases like:

"campgrounds near me"
"[City] camping"
"RV parks [State]"
"[Campground name]"
Leverage Google Keyword Planner for volume data.

Subsection 1.4: Landing Pages

Send traffic to tailored landing pages highlighting your amenities, activities, accommodations and easy booking process.

Subsection 1.5: Budgets and Bidding

Set daily budgets aligned with targets; increase budgets gradually as you track conversion performance. Use automated bidding strategies.

Section 2: Social Media Advertising

Sponsored posts and ads allow you to geo-target nearby travelers on major social platforms.

Subsection 2.1: Facebook & Instagram Ads

Create ads optimized for placement across:

Facebook News Feed

Facebook Stories
Instagram Feed
Instagram Stories
Target by location radius, age, interests, and behaviors.

Subsection 2.2: Ad Creative and Formats

Develop ad creative that stops scrollers. Use:

Captivating HD visuals - campground views, amenities, activities
Video ads showcasing property and grounds
Carousels with multiple graphics and captions
Clear, engaging captions and calls-to-action
Subsection 2.3: Other Platforms

Consider paid campaigns on Snapchat, Pinterest, Twitter, and TikTok. Test performance for your audience.

Subsection 2.4: Budgets and Auctions

Set daily or lifetime budgets per campaign. Bid competitively based on your cost per conversion target.

Section 3: Display Advertising

Display ads promote brand visibility across thousands of websites.

Subsection 3.1: Google Display Network

The Google Display Network offers:

Site-targeted text, image, and video ads
Advanced audience targeting
Remarketing to past visitors
Subsection 3.2: Website Ads

Buy direct ads on niche sites frequented by your audience like:

Outdoor and adventure travel blogs
Family vacation sites
RV enthusiast websites

Local event calendars
Subsection 3.3: Video Ads

Run pre-roll, mid-roll, and bumper video ads on YouTube, social media, and across video publisher networks.

Subsection 3.4: Tracking and Optimization

Track key metrics like impressions, clicks, and conversions. Adjust targeting and creative based on performance.

Section 4: Travel Advertising

Reach travelers researching trips through key travel sites and partners.

Subsection 4.1: Tripadvisor

Enhance your Tripadvisor presence through:

Sponsored placement in search results
Additional photo slots
Branded content campaigns
Book on Tripadvisor partner program
Subsection 4.2: Hotel and Booking Sites

List your property and advertise on Booking.com, Hotels.com, etc. Commissions apply for referrals.

Subsection 4.3: Travel Publishers

Buy ads or sponsored content on travel blogs and magazines like Lonely Planet, Travel & Leisure, and more.

Subsection 4.4: Influencer Partnerships

Collaborate on sponsored content with camping influencers who align with your brand.

Section 5: Direct Mail Advertising

Although digital advertising dominates, direct mail can still effectively nurture leads and past customers when targeted well.

Consider:

Personalized promotion mailers to nearby households
Postcard campaigns highlighting seasonal packages or events
Loyalty rewards programs for repeat guests
Special occasion cards and partner promotions
Track redemption rates to gauge ROI. Mail selectively to optimize spend.

Conclusion

This chapter provided a comprehensive overview of today's top paid advertising options for campgrounds to reach motivated travelers across multiple digital channels and traditional direct mail. Key takeaways include:

Search ads capture those ready to book
Social ads boost local brand awareness
Display ads broaden exposure across niche sites
Travel platform ads intercep booking journeys
Direct mail nurtures existing relationships
Carefully testing select paid channels aligned to your audience and business goals allows you to control your brand visibility and acquisition efforts. Continually optimize based on performance data to maximize your ad investment.

Paid advertising works hand in hand with organic marketing to attract and convert the right campers for your property. With a sound paid strategy, you can scale your reach and revenue.

CHAPTER 8: SPECIAL EVENTS AND PROMOTIONS

Introduction

Special events and promotions are invaluable for generating excitement, attendance, and revenue for campgrounds. Well-executed occasions give current campers more reasons to visit and give potential guests a taste of your hospitality.

This chapter will provide tactics to:

Plan memorable events aligned with your brand and audience
Select the right promotional offers to maximize bookings
Promote events and deals through online and offline channels
Recruit sponsors and vendors to cover costs
Manage event logistics to delight attendees
Measure results through surveys, sales data, and web analytics
Follow this playbook to make events and promotions cornerstones of your annual marketing calendar.

Section 1: Popular Campground Events

Brainstorm interactive events suited to your amenities, season, and guests. Consider:

Subsection 1.1: Holiday Weekends

Extend stays around peak holidays like July 4th, Labor Day, and Memorial Day with activities like:

Fireworks shows
Decked out campsite competitions
Holiday crafts and games
Themed food and cocktails
Subsection 1.2: Outdoor Movie Nights

Offer family-friendly entertainment through outdoor movie screenings. Encourage costumes, sell snacks.

Subsection 1.3: Wine/Beer/Food Events

Partner with wineries, breweries, food trucks or restaurants for tasting events showcasing local fare.

Subsection 1.4: Kids' Activity Days

Keep kids engaged with scavenger hunts, crafts, obstacle courses, educational activities about nature and wildlife native to your area.

Subsection 1.5: Pet-Friendly Happenings

For dog-loving guests, arrange pet parades, contests, professional photos with pets, and vendors catering to pet goods/services.

Section 2: Planning Successful Events

Proper planning ensures events run smoothly while achieving goals.

Subsection 2.1: Setting Goals

Define what success looks like before planning:

Attendance numbers
Revenue targets
Brand visibility objectives
Subsection 2.2: Timeline and Checklists

Outline detailed timelines listing all milestones from concept to event wrap-up:

Initial brainstorming
Sponsor recruitment
Marketing rollout
Vendor and entertainment booking
Logistical arrangements
Post-event analysis
Subsection 2.3: Promotion

Market events through:

Website banners and event pages
Social media campaigns
Email promotions and newsletters
Online event calendars
Print signage and flyers on property and locally
Subsection 2.4: Partnerships

Partner with vendors and sponsors to fund events in exchange for marketing exposure. Ideas include:

Activity providers offering demos
Food/beverage suppliers
Event rental and supply companies
Local attractions and businesses
Community partners
Section 3: Promotions to Boost Visits

Strategic offers incentivize bookings during lower demand periods.

Subsection 3.1: Discounts and Coupons

Highlights include:

Parents stay free with kids
25% off Sunday overnight stays
$50 off 2 nights or more
BOGO Half Off summer weekdays
Subsection 3.2: Free Time Offers

For example:

Stay 4 nights, get 1 free
Free night with qualifying activities
Book 3 weekends, get 1 weekend free
Subsection 3.3: Loyalty Programs

Offer perks through point or punch card programs, like a free site upgrade after 5 stays.

Subsection 3.4: Packaged Deals

Bundle accommodations with amenities like bike rentals, event tickets, or dining vouchers.

Subsection 3.5: Contests and Giveaways

Encourage shares, follows, and bookings for prize entries. For instance, free stays for summer Instagram photo contest winners.

Section 4: Analyzing Results

Measure success and identify areas for improvement.

Subsection 4.1: Event Attendance

Track:

Site occupancy during events
Event ticket sales if applicable
Concessions and vendor revenue
Subsection 4.2: Promotion Redemption Rates

Code promotions to track usage and gauge ROI.

Subsection 4.3: Digital Engagement

Assess social media, email, and website analytics around events and offers:

Exposure and reach
Clickthrough and conversion rates

Use of branded hashtags
Subsection 4.4: Attendee Surveys

Solicit feedback on satisfaction, likelihood to return, and suggested improvements.

Conclusion

Memorable events and strategic offers provide compelling reasons to visit your campground. They showcase your hospitality in action. Use this chapter's tips to brainstorm, plan, promote, execute, and optimize occasions tailored to your guests. Add energy to your marketing program and valued incentives that make booking easy and rewarding.

The key is understanding your audience. With creative events tied to their interests and discounts addressing pain points, you give potential guests every reason to choose your campground as their homebase for adventure and relaxation.

CHAPTER 9: CUSTOMER RETENTION

Introduction

Acquiring new customers is important, but retaining existing ones is essential for campground profitability over time. Repeat visitors spend more, require less marketing costs to attract, and promote your property through word-of-mouth referrals.

This chapter will explore proven tactics to foster loyalty and lasting relationships with guests, including:

Collecting visitor data to inform personalized communications
Developing rewards programs that make guests feel valued
Ongoing transactional and engagement communications via email
Monitoring satisfaction metrics and online reviews
Hosting special events just for loyal guests
Follow this playbook to make customer retention central to your campground marketing strategy.

Section 1: Collecting Visitor Data

Robust customer data enables personalized communications that deepen loyalty. Capture information through:

Subsection 1.1: Reservations and Check-In

Request key details at booking:

Home address
Email address
Phone number
Number and age of guests
Special occasions
Upon check-in, confirm details and add:

Site number
License plate
Activities planned
Subsection 1.2: Site Usage and Engagement

Note each guest's on-site behaviors:

Amenities used - pools, trails, rec areas
Areas visited
Retail purchases
Service requests
Cross-reference with reservations data.

Subsection 1.3: Post-Stay Surveys

Send email surveys asking about their experience and satisfaction. Offer incentives for completion.

Subsection 1.4: Reviews and Social Media

If guests leave public feedback, capture their comments for research. Monitor social media engagement.

Section 2: Building Loyalty Programs

Programs that make guests feel valued and offer exclusive perks inspire lasting affinity.

Subsection 2.1: Points-Based Rewards

Award points for actions like:

Visits
Referrals

Reviews
Retail purchases
Renewing newsletter subscription
Let points be redeemed for free nights, upgrades, merchandise, etc.

Subsection 2.2: Punch Card Rewards

Alternatively, offer paper or digital punch cards:

Buy 10 get 1 free night
10 site night visits = free upgrade
Subsection 2.3: Tiered Status Levels

Define member levels, like Bronze, Silver, and Gold, with ascending benefits. Make it easy to move up tiers.

Subsection 2.4: Rewarding Behavior

In addition to free stays, reward desired behavior with perks like:

Early check-in/late checkout
Free WiFi
Bonus loyalty points
Merchandise gifts
Free amenities
Subsection 2.5: Status Recognition

Make loyal guests feel valued through special touches like:

Addressed by name at check-in
Welcome signs on their site
Special badges on site maps
Exclusive member merchandise
Section 3: Ongoing Communications

Consistency builds familiarity and trust. Stay top of mind through:

Subsection 3.1: Confirmations and Pre-Arrival Tips

Send booking confirmations and pre-arrival emails with trip-planning tips.

Subsection 3.2: Post-Stay Surveys

Solicit feedback via online surveys to uncover pain points and improve experiences.

Subsection 3.3: Thank You Emails

Follow up each stay by thanking guests and inviting reviews. Demonstrate you value their business.

Subsection 3.4: Transactional Messages

Send seamless reservation updates, reminders, invoices and receipts via automated emails.

Section 4: Ongoing Engagement

Non-promotional relationship-building communications provide value.

Subsection 4.1: Email Newsletters

Send monthly newsletters covering topics like:

Renovations and upgrades
New amenities
Staff highlights
Awards or media features
Sneak peeks at events
Subsection 4.2: Special Offers

Surprise members with exclusive savings around:

Birthdays
Loyalty program milestones
New amenity launches
Local area happenings
Subsection 4.3: Appreciation Events

Host member events like complimentary happy hours, potlucks, or campfires solely for your repeat guests.

Section 5: Monitoring Satisfaction

Track metrics revealing loyalty levels to address issues.

Subsection 5.1: Survey Response Rates

High response rates to post-stay surveys indicate engaged members. Low response may signal dissatisfaction.

Subsection 5.2: Review Monitoring

Favorable online reviews reflect member satisfaction. Address poor reviews immediately.

Subsection 5.3: Net Promoter Score

Gauge willingness to recommend via NPS survey question. Score above 50 is favorable.

Subsection 5.4: Repeat Visits and Churn

Calculate percentage of repeat annual visits versus new visitors. Monitor churn rate.

Conclusion

By collecting robust customer data and consistently nurturing relationships through communications, perks, and appreciation, campgrounds inspire lasting loyalty and retention. This chapter provided strategies for:

Capturing visitor details to inform personalized outreach

Developing rewards programs that make guests feel valued

Maintaining ongoing interactions through surveys, newsletters and offers

Monitoring key satisfaction metrics and swiftly addressing issues

Hosting special member events to foster community

Getting retention right means your best customers continually market and refer new guests through word-of-mouth. A thriving base of brand advocates drives growth exponentially.

CHAPTER 10:
ANALYTICS AND KPIS

Introduction

Data drives strategic decision making and optimization for campground owners. Robust analytics provide visibility into your marketing performance, growth trends, reputation, and achievement of key objectives.

This chapter will explore essential metrics and reporting tools to:

Track marketing campaign effectiveness across channels like website, email, social media, advertising, and more

Monitor key business health indicators including occupancy, RevPAR, revenue, costs, and profitability

Manage your online reputation through review sentiment analysis and surveys

Set strategic KPIs for marketing and business growth, with goal setting frameworks and performance tracking

Follow this comprehensive guide to embed insightful measurement and data analysis into your campground marketing and management. Optimize efforts, margins, and experiences powered by key insights.

Section 1: Marketing Performance Analytics

Measure marketing impact across every channel to identify what works.

Subsection 1.1: Website Analytics

Platforms like Google Analytics provide data on:

Traffic volume by source
Site content engagement
On-site conversions and sales
Optimization opportunities
Subsection 1.2: Email Marketing Analytics

Email service providers report on:

Open and clickthrough rates
Conversion tracking by campaign
List growth and engagement over time
Subsection 1.3: Social Media Analytics

Each platform supplies analytics on:

Followers and follower growth
Content impressions and reach
Engagement rates by post
Link clicks and website referrals
Subsection 1.4: Advertising Analytics

Ad platforms give data on:

Impressions and reach
Clicks, CTRs, and costs
Conversions by campaign
Attribution modeling
Section 2: Business Performance Metrics

Key metrics demonstrate campground financial health and growth.

Subsection 2.1: Revenue and RevPAR

Calculate:

Overall gross revenue

Revenue per Available Site (RevPAR)
Revenue segmented by source - sites, retail, F&B
Benchmark against past performance and goals.

Subsection 2.2: Occupancy Rates

Measure:

Overall occupancy percentage
Peak vs. off-season occupancy
Weekend vs. weekday occupancy
High, consistent occupancy indicates demand.

Subsection 2.3: Average Daily Rate

Track your average nightly rate over time. Maintain optimal ADR balancing occupancy.

Subsection 2.4: Ancillary Revenue

Calculate sales from extras like:

Retail
Food and beverage
Equipment rentals
Activity fees
Subsection 2.5: Operating Costs and Profit

Factor costs to determine actual profitability. Control costs to maximize margins.

Section 3: Online Reputation Management

Your online presence and mentions impact prospective guests.

Subsection 3.1: Review Monitoring

Track review volume, ratings, and sentiment on platforms like Google, TripAdvisor, and Facebook.

Subsection 3.2: Responding to Reviews

Reply to all reviews thanking guests. Follow up on any poor

reviews to resolve issues.

Subsection 3.3: Surveys

Send post-stay surveys to collect feedback directly from recent guests.

Subsection 3.4: Social Media Monitoring

Monitor brand mentions and conversations on social media. Join relevant local community groups.

Subsection 3.5: Competitive Benchmarking

Compare your metrics against competing campgrounds' performance.

Section 4: Setting Strategic KPIs

Key Performance Indicators keep focus on top goals and benchmarks.

Subsection 4.1: Marketing KPIs

Establish and monitor KPIs like:

Website visits
Email subscriber growth
Social media followers
Online bookings
Advertising conversions
Subsection 4.2: Business KPIs

Set targets for metrics like:

Occupancy rates
RevPAR
Average daily rate
Repeat reservation percentage
Revenue growth
Subsection 4.3: Selecting KPIs

Identify 3-5 KPIs that reflect your core goals, like site nights booked, first-time guest conversion, or Google rating.

Subsection 4.4: Goal Setting

Set specific, measurable goals for each KPI, like increasing website conversion rate by 25% quarter-over-quarter.

Subsection 4.5: Performance Tracking

Monitor KPIs through a dashboard. Review periodically against goals.

Conclusion

Data and insights uncover key opportunities for campgrounds - from refining underperforming marketing channels to capitalizing on popular amenities and high-value offers. This chapter provided best practices for:

Tracking marketing analytics across digital channels
Monitoring business health metrics and profitability
Managing your online reputation through active review responses and surveys
Setting strategic KPIs tied to core objectives, with rigorous performance tracking
With comprehensive analytics foundations in place, you can confidently identify successful initiatives to expand, and troubleshoot areas needing optimization. Ultimately data visibility enables smart decision making to accelerate campground growth and excellence.

CHAPTER 11: CONCLUSION

We've reached the end of our comprehensive guide to campground marketing. By now, you should feel equipped with actionable strategies and best practices to dramatically grow your campground's visibility, leads, and bookings.

This conclusion summarizes the core concepts and takeaways from each chapter. Let's recap the marketing blueprint covered:

Your campground website is the hub of your digital presence. We discussed how to optimize user experience through clear branding, easy site navigation, compelling content highlighting activities and amenities, strong calls-to-action, and seamless online booking integration. Apply search engine optimization techniques onsite and through link building to improve search visibility. Update and enhance the site regularly to keep attracting visitors.

Social media allows you to engage directly with current and potential guests daily. Maintain active presences on core platforms like Facebook and Instagram where you can share photos, news, special offers, and rich content that inspires travelers. Promote through both organic and paid tactics. Fuel word-of-mouth through user-generated content and influencer marketing.

Forge strategic local partnerships with businesses relevant to your guests like activity providers, restaurants, shops, tourism boards and more. Collaborate on co-marketing campaigns like packages and cross-promotions to generate new leads. Sponsor local events that help raise your community profile.

Email marketing helps nurture relationships with prospects and past guests through valuable, relevant communications. Grow your subscriber list and send targeted campaigns like promotions, newsletters, surveys, and more at strategic times to drive bookings. Automate post-stay reviews and win-back emails to inactive subscribers.

Paid advertising lets you control brand visibility by putting messaging in front of motivated audiences. Experiment with search, social media, travel platform, and display ads. Track conversions to maximize your ad spend across channels.

Memorable events and strategic offers give guests more reasons to visit, while showcasing your campground's signature hospitality. Plan activities aligned with your brand and amenities like holiday weekends, movie nights, or ice cream socials. Offer discounts, free add-ons, and package deals to incentivize bookings during slower periods.

Customer retention is critical, as repeat guests visit more and have higher lifetime value. Collect visitor data to inform personalized communications post-stay. Develop loyalty programs that make guests feel appreciated through points, perks, and special events. Monitoring satisfaction metrics helps you identify issues before they churn visitors.

Robust analytics provide the visibility needed to optimize marketing initiatives and campground operations. Track performance of digital campaigns through website, email, social media, and advertising platforms. Monitor key business health metrics like revenue, occupancy, costs and profit. Manage online reputation through reviews and surveys. Set strategic KPIs to align efforts with overarching growth goals.

After reading this book, you now have a 360-degree view of

proven marketing tactics to make your campground impossible for travelers to ignore online, build lasting guest relationships, provide incredible on-site experiences, and operate profitably.

Here are 3 key overarching takeaways to anchor your campground marketing approach going forward:

Adopt an Omni-Channel Strategy - Orchestrate marketing across your website, social platforms, emails, advertising channels, events, and partnerships for maximum visibility.

Build Relationships and Community - Provide value, privileges and VIP experiences to make guests feel connected to your campground.

Track and Optimize Campaigns - Rigorously monitor performance analytics to double down on what works well. Identify and improve underperforming areas.

If you commit to a long-term, data-driven marketing approach focused on delivering value to guests and community, your campground will thrive.

This concludes our comprehensive guide to campground marketing strategies designed to drive growth. Now it's time to review key sections, begin implementing high-impact tactics, and monitor your results. Experiment iteratively to determine optimal strategies tailored for your property and guests.

Best of luck cultivating the visibility, leads and bookings your campground deserves! Please reach out if I can be a resource as you being executing your marketing plan.

ABOUT THE AUTHOR

Brian Searl

Brian Searl is the founder and CEO of Insider Perks and Modern Campground, leveraging technology and innovation to transform marketing for the outdoor hospitality industry.

With over a decade of experience leading his companies, Brian has established himself as an expert in digital marketing, AI, automation, and data analytics. He takes a creative yet strategic approach, obsessing over the details to help campground and RV park clients boost brand visibility, engagement, and bookings.

When he's not immersed in the tech world, you can find Brian hiking, exploring the great outdoors, or spending time with his beloved Yorkshire Terrier, Rylee.

Brian is passionate about customer service and growth. He constantly reinvests profits to improve offerings and has become a recognized thought leader through appearances at industry events and his weekly podcast, MC Fireside Chats.

Ready to take your campground marketing to the next level? Get in touch with Brian to discuss how his personalized, forward-thinking strategies can increase your revenue and set you apart from the competition.